WAYMARKS

JAMES THORNTON

WAYMARKS

JAMES THORNTON

Published by Barbican Press, London and Los Angeles

Copyright © James Thornton, 2022

Registered office: 1 Ashenden Road, London E5 0DP

www.barbicanpress.com

@barbicanpress1

Photo of a Joshua Tree by Wei Zeng / Unsplash

Design by Jason Anscomb.

A CIP catalogue for this book is available from
the British Library

ISBN: 978-1-909954-51-9

Typeset in Palatino

Typeset in India by Imprint Press

Printed and bound by CPI Group (UK) Ltd, Croydon, CR0 4YY

For Martin

Biography

The New Statesman named James Thornton as one of 10 people who could change the world. Irish-American, James is also the author of *Client Earth* (Scribe 2018), co-authored with his husband Martin Goodman, which received the Judges' Selection, Business Book of the Year Award 2018, and the Green Prize for Sustainable Literature from Santa Monica Public Library. He has twice won Leader of the Year at the Business Green Awards. James is a Zen Buddhist priest, and founder and president of ClientEarth, the leading global not-for-profit law group. For his legal work, *The Financial Times* awarded him its Lifetime Achievement Award. He lives in London and Los Angeles.

'James Thornton speaks as both a poet who has colonised science and a scientist who speaks a poetic tongue.'

– E.O. Wilson

'James Thornton is a poet of deep wisdom and love!'

– Satish Kumar

Praise for James's previous two collections, *The Feynman Challenge* and *Notes from a Mountain Village*:

'Weaves quiet perception and poignant reflection on humans, animals, and landscape into a shimmering pattern of southern French light.'

– Olafur Eliasson

'A poignant and evocative paean to an ancient village high in the French Pyrenees, where the reinvigorating miracle of the natural world is tinged with reflections on mortality.'

– Homero Aridjis

'This is a generous book, happy to serve the curiosity, the wonder and humility of science, happening here and there in words that simply send a shudder – *Two black holes are about / to marry, a billion years ago* – through our sense of time and space.'

– Philip Gross

Introduction

People take selfies when they travel. I do too, but also make poems to capture an inside reflection of who this person was then.

These poems were written over lots of miles and years. You'll meet a number of characters. Sometimes it's clear from the description who they are, like the Belgian millionaire at dinner, the Chinese supreme court judge, or the beggar in the Beijing airport.

Sometimes they're named, and I'd like to briefly introduce these *dramatis personae*.

The first is *Martin* my husband, who is 'you' in a number of poems, and named in a couple of others.

Ram Dass was an American spiritual teacher. Earlier in life he was known as Dr Richard Alpert, when he taught psychology at Harvard. Together with Timothy Leary he launched the '60s psychedelic movement in America, then went on to study in India and became a spiritual teacher in his own right.

Poonja was one of the leading Indian sages of the 20th century. Regarded as a jivanmukta or liberated being, he taught Self-inquiry, a rigorous form of practice, in the tradition of Ramana Maharshi. Students from around the world came to visit him at a humble house in Lucknow.

Maezumi Roshi was a seminal figure in bringing Zen from Japan to the West. Oxford University Press's scholarly *Zen Masters* studies him as one of the 10 significant figures in Zen history. He founded the Zen Center of Los Angeles, and began a lineage of Western Zen teachers. He was my own teacher for some ten years.

James Broughton was an American poet and filmmaker. He was a figure in the San Francisco Renaissance, which prefigured the Beats. He specialized in breaking boundaries, setting out the challenges of freedom to younger writers, and encouraging them on their way.

In this German Village

Thalheim, Germany

Winter in this German village:
I'm on a retreat
in the house of an Indian holy woman
who lives here.

I lie awake in the dark
listening alone to the owl
and the church bell's quarter hours.

Your letter was full of anger
and I worry you will leave me.
But my sadness is stronger:
feeling your pain, knowing I cannot remove it.

Sometimes

Dorndorf, Germany

Sometimes, when an old woman
in a soft carapace of fat
exuded over decades
by despair, looks up
with the eye of a girl
from her piece of cake

Sometimes, when a friend
who's dying of the virus
whose falling-out teeth
I'd find on the nightstand
who can't walk further
stops and says, "I've missed
until now, how each day
is full of wonder"

Sometimes, when we
through unfathomed grace
find the reverence
to enter the sanctuary
of another's subjectivity

We remember we are children
But we are always children
and must remember and remember
and remember until we
sleep in death and wake

Meteors

Thalheim, Germany

Late night walk between two towns
in the German countryside

investigating my relationship
with the material world

I look up at the sky
and ask for a shooting star

and there is a shooting star
I ask for another
and there is another

the game continues till five
have burned across the dark

I laugh
not because I believe I've commanded them
into being
but for the flow, the play

Unnameable

Thalheim, Germany

On this same road between two towns
in daylight

I saw behind
the canvas on which the world
is painted into familiar shapes

shapes we name and manage
shapes we've evolved to see

this canvas was drawn back and I saw
the unfocused

the unnameable the unmanageable
shapes before form
world before name
the source before we collapse it into things

it was welcoming
it was beckoning
it was vibrant warmth and colour

then the canvas dropped back in place
world become things again

Kali

Thalheim, Germany

In the September sun filled
garden, soft and black
you nuzzle me.

I call you Kali
and ask to learn of
birth and death.

All at once you stalk
and pounce
play long enough
to let me near:

Small bones crunch softly
entrails mauve and tan
licked clean and left
to quiver on the lawn.

The grass is green
the sunlight gold
the air ripe apple filled.

You look up heavy-lidded
insatiable
and note the thrush in the lilac.

Purring again, you come
and nuzzle me
soft and black
and I call you Kali.

Poonja

San Francisco

Preparing to go to India, I ran into Ram Dass
at a San Francisco party
in the house of a rich man

As we ate big prawns on skewers we spoke:
"I want to meet a guru in India, who should it be?"
"There is a man there called Poonja, find him!"

I found him in Lucknow and joined
the queue for his satsang
then sitting face to face
before his large daily audience I said:

"Bliss often comes unbidden
catches me unawares
and has a thousand subtle variations.
But it also brings pain
since what's bliss and what's not
is so much sharper now."

"You're wrong!" he shouted.
"Now that you know bliss
your pain is only bubbles
of old habits rising up.

10

Observe them as they rise
and you'll discover
that even these
are coated now with bliss!"

I bowed to thank him
and he bowed back.

Dharamshala

India

The butterfly was white
in heavy sunlight
behind his head.

He'd charged into the room
chimera of lion and woman
we talked in his study
more than an hour
of my practice, of overpopulation
overconsumption
planetary ills then
the Dalai Lama
asked me to teach.

"You must become confident
and positive and help
others to become
confident and positive
the solutions we need
can never emerge
from angry minds."

In Roshi's study

Los Angeles

I travelled back from Dharamshala to LA
sat in the private study
of my Zen teacher Maezumi Roshi

And eagerly shared
the message the Dalai Lama gave me:

You must become confident and positive
and help others to become
confident and positive
the solutions we need
can never emerge from angry minds

And Roshi said
"That's basic Buddhism."

Five on returning to California broke at 43

Carpinteria, California

1.

I've just come halfway
around the world
France to California
arriving here tired
and broke
overwhelmed
with a feeling of failure.
I'm 43, no job
but mortgage due
my patient hard work
these years unrewarded
and I remember:
Give us this day
our daily bread
and hang hard onto that thought.

2.

No job no money
but I have these:
a good relationship
with my man
and with my family
a good book written
still unpublished
another in draft
piles of poems
and this:
I've cast off the ties
that bound me
to institutions and people
who used me
and have found
the deepest place.
So I tell myself: my worries
are only practical problems.

3.

This feeling there is
so much to pour out
and I am aging and
distracted by money worries.

It's true and false:
True that there is
nectar to gather
in my heart and mind.
False too: when
I worry, it's the worry
not the need for money
that stops me.

4.

How easily annoyed I am
these last few days
with those who love me most.
Under it, I see how angry
I am with the world
that it won't easily accept
the gifts I want to give it.
But what can I expect?
I want to wake it up.
How will I survive
if I make my happiness
depend on being listened to?

5.

In the Pinte du Nord
our cheap Paris hotel
Martin said to me
before we parted:
"You are a spiritual teacher
who writes, I am
a writer who conveys
spiritual teachings
you need only share
what you already are
and let the wind of
heaven dance between us."

Morning walk with pelicans

Carpinteria, California

A morning walk with pelicans
seven in line
ride the green impermanent edge
of a near shore wave
till it falls upon itself
and the just risen Sun
turns the roil to frothing milk

They rise in sequence
to drop on the next wave
arcing and gliding on

A line from Welsh poet R S Thomas
returns to mind:
Why do I love them?
They are beautiful, millions of years old
and never harm the Earth

Barstow, CA

Dehydrated tonight
in Barstow CA.

The British election's
ten days away.

My mind shifting
from global to local
and back.

Here in the desert
as in Britain, people
see only what's before them.

We don't understand
our way of life ravages
the web of life.

That will come
like all wisdom
after we've
suffered a fair return
for our actions.

Desert tortoise

Joshua Tree National Park, California

A friend tells me Joshua Tree with its billowy rocks
and spiky lilies tall as trees
is the most beautiful place on Earth

I walk into its desert
climbing boulder hills
looking for a place to sit and fast

Come to a hillside and stay there
sit and let the day fill me
then find

My neighbour is a desert tortoise
perched at the edge of her burrow
meditating

As we sit together I pray that she
unlike many of her rapidly vanishing kin
will not be smashed by a 4x4

On visiting The Huntington Library

Pasadena, California

The aesthetic of a culture
can reside in a single tree.

Consider the Japanese split-
leaved maple:
Leaf plane a minimum gesture
fringed out in seven veins,
the whole odd numbered
yet radially symmetric.

Leaf sharply defined;
tree hazy at the edges.
While the leaves' oxblood
red pleasingly disappoints
the expectation
of green.

Walnut Creek

California

I see the reflections
in the mirror
in the sushi bar.
Everything seems clearer
in a glass.

I've entered the USA
on my Irish passport.
I'm a refugee in England
because my lover isn't allowed
to live here. I'm not home
anymore in the USA
here in the USA.

I've left to love
far from here
my only home now the UK
I can no longer see home
be at home
here in the USA
here in the USA.

I look out at the gas guzzlers
that people here with
heart breaking stupidity
think are patriotic.

I drink more sake
look in the mirror
and see we are hurting
ourselves into the future
like light into a black hole.

Bridger Teton Wilderness 1

Wyoming

Can we throw off all our peeves
our suffering and pain
lifelong though we've cherished them
our dramas and everything else
we hold tight against the world
and let love pour through
the love that's always there

Will it surprise us will we find
it is completely impersonal
yet what we've always wanted

Bridger Teton Wilderness 2

Wyoming

In wildernesss we're in
our true body manifest

I've seen bald eagles and osprey today
tasted wild strawberries
in a mountain wood
and felt with my whole body
the wisdom encoded in Nature
which proliferates when undisturbed

Today also brought this: living in cities we are
with our whole bodies absorbing madness

Bridger Teton Wilderness 3

Wyoming

The waters of this mountain lake slap
its shore in languid foreplay
its surface condenses sunlight
till wavepeaks shatter like mirrors do

The expression on the waters
registers the shifting play of wind
with a dancer's finesse

I sense all at once
the whole lake's alive
like a single great jellyfish
filling this glaciated granite bowl

Bridger Teton Wilderness 4

Wyoming

Four elements prayer:

Give me the power of water
that melts away stones
to change the minds of people

The power of fire
to fill their hearts
with inspiration

The power of wind
to move healing ideas
through minds across the globe

And the power of Earth
to nurture and sustain
a new ecological civilization

Port Townsend with James Broughton

Washington State

I told him, "I hear a music
that makes a shape
only words can fill."
And he said, "you, my dear
are hereby condemned
to the ecstasies
and all the rigors
of poetry. Persevere.

You'll find there is no end
of subjects and that language
invents itself. When
language makes itself
intimately new through you.
Your life flowers
that is your blossoming
and perfection."

Broughton's Blessing

Port Townsend, Washington

For you, he said, there will be no end
of subjects or inspiration.
Poetry is to language
as the first kiss is to love.

The more you write the more there'll be to draw on
and the more fluidly your voice will flow.
And remember this always:
a memorable line redeems a day.

Cedar

Olympic Peninsula, Washington

In the rainforest
west of Seattle
a single ancient cedar
dead a thousand years
made me stop for worship
more moving
because more live
than Chartres

Olympic Rain Forest

Washington

Hands deep in green moss pelt
on ancient fir
wind's voice pulls me
two hundred feet up
till I feel wind's gentle caress
with my every needle
then suddenly
I'm drawn deep down
by the tenacious
ramiculation of my roots

An Alaskan Sutra

Anchorage to Denali

Sunglints in dew on orbwebs of the taiga
offer praise
Drakes paddling virgin ponds unsullied
offer praise
Moose plodding shy and aggressive
offer praise
The bear and the salmon in its gullet
offer praise
The eagle and the air that shapes its flight
offer praise
The snowskin on Denali, great sacred mountain
offers praise
Each of them independently
offers praise
and also together
in their oneness with you
with me with us all
offer their praise ceaselessly

Chapin Bay Alaska

pores open in the water's
skin: raindrops

water's body pulses with lion's mane jellyfish
and their poison draglines

into the old pines
ravens float their croaks

Denali

Alaska

Taiga

puffballs in muskeg
bear prints in glacial milk
a raptor's shadow

Tundra

struggling step by step
kettlepond reflects mountain peaks
golden eagle skull

Sukoi Inlet Alaska

The mirror stretched taut
by gravity reflects the sky
with easy accuracy
until broken
by leaping salmon
whose ripples soon
extenuate to level.

The rising Sun polishes
the restored mirror
while from a snag
the eagle watches.

Canoe

Alaska

A congregation of intimates
we're back in Alaska

to memorialize our friend
who liked trees better than people

wilderness Alaska
his place of worship

My canoe glides across
yellow starfish near the shore

pushes past seaweed islands
suburbs for otters

Near the opposite shore clouds
of mosquitos

but worth a blood tithe to sit near
red-necked phalaropes

then far out
the only bird who crosses

the North Pacific
that little auk

the Ancient Murrelet

Ram Dass

Berkeley, California

After he had his stroke
I visited him
at his rambling place in Berkeley
The porch door was open
he called from his bedroom
so I crossed the living room
his energetic paintings
piled against each other
along the walls

He was resting in bed
smiling
behind his moustache
I spent the afternoon with him
having tea, cosily chatting
about psychedelics and masters

He pronounced that one of my friends
was 'smart,' another 'strong'
and that I was 'good'
I wondered if I was satisfied with that
but he'd moved on
to talk about his stroke

He called it "heavy grace,"
and while it slowed him down
he worked with it
"When I want to find words,"
he said, "I surf the silence"

By San Francisco Bay

the world ocean
the one moon
opposite sides of the planet
still connected

Banded Peak Ranch

Northern New Mexico

Where riffling stream
caresses tender breast of Earth
and trees breathe free
in empty space made blue by air
I sink happy again
into all my senses
We have so little time

March of the Sandhill Cranes

Bosque del Apache, New Mexico

It's cold sleeping
standing all night
in water in the winter
but safe from coyotes.

Gray against the dawn
we walk silent
stillness moving as ones and twos
as groups and long slow lines.

The raucous young
for whom their wings are new
will jump and stamp and
spread those wings in fleeting dance
then join the rest
to limber cold limbs
by marching in slow cadence
to the dawn's soft silence.

When our time comes
we lower our necks
think ourselves to flight
and trumpet the new day.

Whooper

Bosque del Apache, New Mexico

There are a thousand or more
standing in a field of corn at their ease
Sandhill cranes

We've watched them over the years as they wake
standing in cold water
limber slowly and fly to feed

Among them at a great distance
as if hiding
or seeking company

the telescope just disclosing
through shimmers heat adds to distant vision
a Whooping crane

Alone among its cousins, white against their grey
out of less than four hundred living wild

Reverently we watch then have to go

New York

I love New York
when it snows
I love New York
when the rain pours down

I love New York
when nature's body
pushes close and
seagulls fill the air

Heat Island

New York

In this life's geography New York
was thirty years ago home.
Now living in London and flying
in from Beijing I meet the city
exuding summer sweat from skin
of buildings and sidewalks' summer smell
from underarms and garbage.

Chicas flaunt it hot so you can
see all the curves, anglo matrons
do it in a less ambitious way
while a black youth softly taunts
the subway crowd flashing his underwear.

From the Brooklyn Diner by Carnegie Hall
the street has emptied of sunlight all at once
a fractional rotation of Earth making
Manhattan a sundial.

For most of the day I've been at Jamaica Bay
bathed in birdsong with honeysuckle and beach rose
scents extracted by our star's heat.

In a few minutes in the hall
Prokofiev's piano and violin sonatas
will elevate, as much as possible,
the noise we make towards
the emptiness of what I think of as real.

A Walk in Central Park

New York

To relieve the pounding skyline
with its traffic obbligato
entered the park

lemon and vermillion leaves
bare branched trees
walked for miles
on paths less followed

found white crowned sparrows
in a house sparrow flock

then a bat flew down
an Eastern red
who hang like leaves during day
blonde mink fur
to lay on the path before me
unmoving

since dogs and their people
would soon happen by
picked her up

took her to an outcrop of ancient igneous
laid her to rest
in last light
said prayers over her

Oyster Bay barn swallows

New York

It didn't take long
to get caught up in their world

Only three can face out
the fourth pushed behind
but they take turns
to defecate gladly over the edge
then rotate to the back

A fifth who left home first
perches undecided
on a nearby ledge

Once and sometimes three times
a minute a parent flashes in
staying on the wing
chooses a noisy mouth to feed
not forgetting the nest leaver

While the parents hunt
the remainers look down
respectfully consider
the ground
and their perhaps fatal move

By next morning
they've all fully finished
fledging and flown

Beacon Hill

Boston, Massachusetts
for Richmond 1997

There are places in cities—Beacon Hill
is one, its undulating brick sidewalks
leotards of baked clay
stretched over the sinuous
roots of trees and muscles of Earth
where we meet
signs of nature's patience
its inevitable ascendency
and the transient body
of all our works

Riding the Boston T

Were we moulds it would be slime
if ciliates, pseudopods we'd extend

Were we squid there'd be
overskin lightshows

If birds, balletic displays
like cranes dancing

We're apes though so I need
not envy those intimacies

In the Boston T today during long delays
I scoped my fellow apes

Appreciated their relaxed
demeanour

Knowing if it were a train full of chimps
we'd be at each others' throats

Regalia 1

Peruvian Amazonia

Last night I lay on the dirt floor
in the ayahusacuero's hut

The old man sang his *icaros*
then the jungle said:
All of life is lovemaking
flirtation, seduction, being eaten
a flowing exchange of energies

With every second of your life
you must make love
the jungle said
And I said yes

Regalia 2

Peruvian Amazonia

The jungle held me soft last night
ayahuasca whispered in my ear:
open every pore to me
let me through your skin
my mammal body cradled frail
relaxed into the jungle's hold
I heard the sound
of these bones breaking
as the gateway to the source

On a gentler ayahuasca wave
I saw myself lie comfortable
curled upon the ground

realized then I saw
my own death
like that of any jungle creature
who passes peaceful

Reciprocity

Peruvian Amazonia

It's quiet in our jungle camp
during daylight hours between
evenings led by the ayahuascero

Today I walked to a stream to find
the son of one of our guides
torturing a stingless bee
shiny black and fat as a bumblebee
by throwing it into the stream to watch it drown

I explained that killing a helpful
harmless creature was not the way to have fun
and rescued the bee

Later I found a large beetle marooned
on its back, struggling to turn over
so I helped and watched it run away

That night we lay on the ground in our circle
after taking the medicine
and listened to the shaman's *icaros*
several hours into the trip
I felt uncomfortable

Like someone was pinning me down
by the arms and by the legs
The feeling left and then
again the feeling of being pinned down

Martin had not heard my adventures
earlier with bee and beetle

After the session, he said he saw
a six foot long bee made of light
that came and held me down
and dropped nectar in my mouth

Next, he said, came a six foot long beetle
also made of light
who held me down
and fed me nectar

Koriwayti

Peruvian Amazonia

When the invitation to madness
rushing at us penetrates
breath, skin and mind
like water enters cloth
and meeting no resistance
floods us
with the sorcery of dark things
to wordless remember
there is a reason for being
guides us through
like a raft shooting rapids
that refuses to capsize.

Machu Picchu

Peru

As I climbed the peak
to the Sun Gate
chewing the local leaves
a door opened unexpected
a vision of how
to change the world
to save it, of how to find
harmony with the Earth again,
and it was very simple: wonder

For what follows wonder
is reverence
and then everything follows gently

Osa Peninsula

Costa Rica

The early Sun moves multicoloured
dragonflies in thousands, more than
a dozen kinds, over the water lettuce
in the lagoon that is mine while I kayak.

In their aqueous youth these ancient insects
with wings like spatchcocked biplanes
wolf down mosquito larvae.
As adults, should water catch them
they're feed for resident snappers.

Reluctant after heavy moonlit fishing
the boat billed night heron opens eyes
to the slip of my paddle. Overhead
howler monkeys push out thuggish cries
while the iguana listens impassive
ready to drop sixty feet if worried by an eagle.

A crested basilisk runs across the water
earning its handle of Jesus Christ lizard.
Then crocodile rises from the reed bed.
You look into his yellow eyes and see no pity there.

Calakmul

Yucatan Peninsula, Mexico

It's conventional to say smoke
that bats leaving their cave
in multitudes look like smoke

At Calakmul in the Yucatan
on New Year's eve
awaiting bats

Their cave door
is at the bottom of a sinkhole
so you're on a cliff looking down

A few emerge
until hundreds of thousands do
in insectile swarm
eddying up

Binoculars on the cave mouth
in close focus show no bats
no individuals

Only pulsing light
in pentagonal tessalations
endlessly renewed
individuals melted into light

Then you see the bat falcon
like a small black and white peregrine
on the cliff face

One bat now
condensed back from light to form
in its claws

On a Pyrenean peak

Pezilla de Conflent, France

Any place becomes a mirror
when we return to it.
In spring atop a Pyrenean peak again
I see what I've renounced

in these last five months just passed:
Hindu devotion, Buddhist practice,
my preferred teachers, any desire
to be one of them myself

human dramas in every form
so almost all my friends,
and my remaining need to meet
society's expectations.

What have I kept?
My freedom
my lover
my wide-eyed sense of wonder.

Avignon

France
after visiting the Palace of the Popes

I.

There's nowhere on Earth
does not deserve its epic
its people praised in song
for courage and achievement.

At the same time
most people in history
live lost in illusion, their lives
made of suffering and longing.

So what is the heart of the song
of every human being?
Not their deeds or their art
which must always be broken by time
but their gorgeous possibility
always boundless and unstained.

This: they are already perfect
no matter who they are
already full of light
and need only open

to know it for themselves
then follow its course to the end.

II.

Yet it's easy to say every person's
already perfect, already full of light
and needs only to open to know it.
How do we follow its course to the end?

Like this: the whole of life, and every
face of it, every prejudice and curse
pomposity and putdown
every thought using "I" as the referent
must be held in the light
to melt like butter in the sun
until we can't be other than kind
even as we make history.

Gstaad to Montreux

Switzerland

From Gstaad to Montreux
on the panoramic train
they've booked me first class
with elderly Swiss who are
also up early on Sunday

I'd come from London to Gstaad
for dinner with millionaires
in a yacht club in the Alps
to further my cause
met a charming contessa
who owns a swathe of Argentina

and now in the early sunlight
Alpine choughs fly by
while hot air balloons
rise slow as jellyfish

Gnomic

Gstaad, Switzerland

The Belgian millionaire
on my left last night with heavy
lipstick and careful hair said:
"I know who you are!"

"In Belgium we have good
gnomes who live in
the woods and wear little
red hats and fix things.
And that's you."

Paris at the Millennium

A couple of wealthy friends have brought us to Paris
to join in a late dinner on the last night of the century.
The food is good the wine even better
my first Yquem from magnum.
The other guests rush out for the stroke of midnight.
I stay to have a quiet glass of Yquem
and tell the waiters they should have some.
Then join the others to watch the lights
on the Eiffel Tower.
Around us on the bridge is reveller detritus.
This being Paris at the millennium it's mostly
empty champagne bottles and their corks.

Via Nassa

Lugano, Switzerland

Summer, Lugano, Via Nassa
after midnight after the event
where I'm raising money
the street's empty as I walk back to my hotel.

The pornography of Switzerland,
the watches, are all put away from shop windows.

The rock concert I've walked past is soft in the distance
no people here now, the street
falling into di Chirico perspective
the street that had to accommodate people all day
now vividly alone
and this is how I like it.

Paris Charles de Gaul

You redeem places
my youth found painful

then why surprized to find myself
with you in Angers

after days walking ancient woods
stalking bluethroat thrush?

In a hotel on my way somewhere
at the end of the day I choose

soft and graceful wine from Anjou
to connect with the Angers morning

and two images overwrite
other memories of the day.

One is news from Warsaw, where the head
of my office phoned to say

the government has fired the Supreme Court
in a move toward fascism.

The balancing image from early in the day
at Gare d'Angers, where we kept waving

till the declination of the pavement
parted us.

Place de Sorbonne

Paris

The kind of evening
in the Place de Sorbonne
when loving the world is easy

The old man stooped to read
the paper over coffee
on his way home

The girls chic and smoking
who pick up my kir bill
when it flutters to the ground

The fellow who bundles his pugs
grundling and snorking
into the fountain for a drink

The two, one old one young,
who ponder difficult texts in the window
of the Librarie Philosophique

And all round
piercing the square from every angle
the young being entirely young

I'm here for a conference with Macron
on a global environment pact

This evening it's easy to stop
worrying for an hour
and enjoy why we want to save it

Brussels dinner

Tonight the Brussels rain
makes the cobblestones fluoresce
green curry raises a sweat on my scalp
while the Labrador barks outside
the Vietnamese hole in the wall
where I've been wondering

why the waiters are distant, look like bouncers
and are heavily tattooed, till the placemat
informs me this eatery is a cell
in a great Asian body offering
"100 percent legal, 100 percent fun"
gambling to the Belgians.

And now the bill tells me
"You've been served by Server."

Brussels morning view

My hotel is a few blocks
from the European Parliament
where I'll be in meetings today

The ivy outside my window
autumn red tendrils on white wall
makes me happy

though not as much
as the foot long
caterpillars in my dream

Tiergarten

Berlin

Sky slightly leaking
I cross the Spree
from the Hauptbahnhof
Reichstag on my left

into the Tiergarten
secure in the knowledge
that a hundred pairs of goshawks
hard to see, barons of the woods

bird eating birds, on rounded wings
working the shapes between branches
hungry for magpie and pigeon
have moved into Berlin.

Meandering, I see a darker grey
against the sky: alert, a master
chest and belly barred, at ease
in a bare tree, ready.

Big birds in Brandenburg

Germany

The plains of Brandenburg
flat and covered with a caul
of northern European sky
were home to innumerable Great Bustards
turkey-sized, heaviest of flying birds.

When a Prussian king called them vermin
they were slaughtered.
He was a nobody
but did lasting damage
to the living world.

They're rare here now.
We find a few in a bare field.
Although it's November a male rehearses
the puffed up dance he'll strut next spring.

In a field nearby, satisfying hordes
of Eurasian cranes, who span northern Europe
to Siberia.

Their tailoring is grey, a black ruff at tail
red patch on crown.

Latin name *Grus grus* sounds like their trumpet calls
that carry three miles

The full-sized yearlings make high-pitched infant calls
still begging for food
and are ignored.

Standing near them in their thousands I'm grateful.

Looking out on Bantry Bay

Ireland

Whether whitecap or gannet
is hard to tell at this height
in low light, squall on
the bay, rainbow just gone.

You can tell when you see one
turn for the plunge, flash white
splash through, finally
bob up, take a leisurely pause
which always make me
think he's made his mark
then fly again.

In fives or sevens they fly by
and make me think of their
sweet work, now part of me.

Off the cliff

Bantry Bay, Ireland

Off the cliff with Bee
just now I dove, and launched
through air in swim
as when I was last Bird.
Not two then, no.

Nettles

Bantry Bay, Ireland

Those nettles that grow
    beyond the garden wall
I've tasted them. Boiled
    they were good.

Those other nettles I've
    reached for all my life
Don't interest me anymore.

Paphos

Cyprus

Listening to the song
of the mountain pines
who would want
to return
to the noise of men?

Unseeable signal

Tenerife, Canary Islands

When you hear canaries wild
you're in the Canaries, where they
supplant house sparrows in hill towns
and are congregational singers

One morning on Mt. Teide
I came to an endemic pine
tall, shaggy, shining in the morning Sun
exuding song

And attended
till on an unseeable signal
yellow shot out in all directions

Barbary falcon

Tenerife, Canary Islands

In the ultramarine air by the sea
in Puerto de la Cruz, one storey up
from our balcony, on the roofline beam,
an artificial cliff, it sits slightly fluffed
but no pigeon, who with canaries
are the common local fowl.

                    The glasses
show a Barbary. He won't often eat
since his meal's nearly his own size
but he'll kill again when hungry, stooping
to hit his prey in flight.

                    We see him fly
from roof to roof to rest and watch then wheel
against the Sun while pigeons flock to shade.

At the close of each day's gambit he streaks
past when sunset loses colour.

                    Below
ten storeys down, two old men keep eight roosts.
They too like to see pigeons breed and fly.

Fuerteventura

Canary Islands

Tonight I ate limpets
hard to scrape off rock
and moray eel, reef predator.

We're on Fuerteventura
a hundred miles off the African coast
and a piece of Spain where Ridley Scott
is making a film of Moses in the desert
a few hundred yards down the beach.

In our short holiday we're both
emerging from our exhaustion
like men gasping for air.

Tonight a gallant waiter served us,
a male couple, some free pink fizz
everyday couples get when they sit down
and made the world a more equal place.

Equal in Extent

Fuerteventura, Canary Islands

Against black volcanic rock
the cinnamon of ruddy shelducks
in a lagoon on Fuerteventura.

Then sitting
in a stone circle to shelter from the wind
body touching Earth's skin
eyes on its horizon
it was obvious for a moment—
the Earth's great span and we
equal in extent, with and of it.

Meanwhile the sea

Lanzarote, Canary Islands

On Lanzarote, desert island off Africa. The waves
pound with Atlantic force against the volcanic coast.
Recovering from overwork, we build joint architec-
tures of memory. We tell stories to recover shared
memory traces. We compare scenes from the plays we
enacted before we shared a stage.

Memories are the stones for building the joint self.
The self that holds while love holds. The self that
holds while health holds. The self that holds while life
holds and before dementia arrives. The joint self that
is the most precious of assets. More important than all
the world's monuments are to history.

Meanwhile in a constant
rhythm the sea pursues its cycles. The sea is welcom-
ing and mothering, I think when I am lively. The sea
is hostile and threatening, I think when I am tired.
Walking into the sea and not coming back would be a
comfort, I think when considering old age and death.
The sea needs my help, I think when climate change
comes to mind.

But the sea has different
thoughts: I am always the same. I am impersonal. It is
your mind that is shifting and changing.

The fisherman of Lake Tana

Ethiopia

The fisherman of Lake Tana
tosses a net
from his papyrus boat
gently penetrating
this water body
source of the Blue Nile.

A giant white pelican
swims along close
just in case.

When the drongo

The Gambia

When the drongo is in the baobob
and the flappet lark percusses its call
When the red hornbill sings goodbye to you
and the Abyssinian roller glides
When the helmet shrike comes out to see you
while the dark chanting goshawk is hunting
When the zitting cisticola's zitting
and the goliath heron is preening
When the honeyguide taunts you to follow
and a turacao is quirkily shy
When the oxpecker sucks down blood and ticks
while a wydah scratches out its living
When common bulbuls play in the garden
and northern crombechs romp in the high leaves
When the hammerkop builds a heavy nest
while the lizard buzzard thinks of reptiles
When a gonolek flashes its scarlet
and the plaintain eater finds a free lunch
When a blue cheeked bee eater pirouettes
and the cameroptera is skulking
When a bearded barbet stays in plain view
and a jacana steps on its lilies

When the eremomela is napping
and the black crake is working at hiding
When the tinker calls out all night long
and the Senegal thick knee looks lively
When the babblers convene and jam loudly
and good news comes to the palm nut vulture
Then you know you're in The Gambia where
during the dry season it gets dusty

The Western Ghats

India

Dawn coming, we park near
the Hindu temple.
Crested swiftlets lined up in a dozen
wake slowly in the architecture.

I watch a big woodpecker
a Greater Flameback:
black, red, and orange
working on its tree hole nest.

A fat priest wearing a skirt
bare chested with big tits
pointedly ignores us as he gets in
his little car and drives off.

Two English Gardens

In a day you can visit
both gardens, if you try.
But it's best to linger in each,
soaking in the life lived there.

The first, backing a Georgian townhouse
built with an eye on bilateral symmetry,
an acre of lawn and ornamentals all correct,
lush and traditional behind high walls,

sits in Rye, near the church,
by the finest house in town,
where he wrote some of his
most important books, Henry James.

And then by bus and steam railway,
a one-third gauge Victorian job
you take for a toy, until you see
the conductor's serious eye,

to the shingle beach at Dungeness,
no trees for miles, only smooth stones, the sea,
fishermen's shacks, and a vast
nuclear power plant advertising tours,

to a small house in the local black,
pertly yellow-trimmed, a garden
of seaside plants, beach stone menhirs,
a bit of Donne in unruly letters on a wall,

and strange sculptures
of rusted bits of iron wrested from the beach,
arranged in ways no waves could have done,
and left to burrow in the mind,

the fragility of life on the severity of shingle,
left open on all sides
to the curious who come now
to Derek Jarman's garden.

I'd envied Henry James, until I
visited his garden, and was discomfited
by its civility. The James I met there
was an unhappy untouchable,

immured behind intricate systems
of rules he found beautifully complex,
the beast's true life in him trapped
behind prose ever more impenetrable,

for it was penetration that he feared above all else.
Jarman, glad for penetration, lived wild,
died young and of aids. What James concealed
to find acceptance, Jarman lived for.

How can we reveal what we are
and find acceptance, or go beyond
the need for it? I hold in my hand a packet
of seeds. It's always the first day of Spring.

Swifts

North London

There were swifts today in Crediton Hill
screaming up and down the street
greedy for the aeolian swarm
airborne bugs delectable
their calls carrying over the
roar of diesel motors
pumping out particles of death
the bird's scream of life
encouraging

Today when I open this poem for an edit
fifteen years on

I read in the paper
swifts were announced
endangered in this country

Music

London South Bank

sometimes it's a bird
trapped in a room   wings
beating the space of panic

sometimes the sky
pushing against itself
grating   moaning

sometimes the risen river
slapping the embankment
caressing   eroding

Crediton Hill

North London

two young men
one black one arab
walk down my street in London

their youthful thrill
in quick bodies and minds

playing back byplay
from their mates
anticipating fun tonight

in that moment so much
do I wish their happiness

against likelihood
my hot tears surprise me

Hampstead Heath

London

Walking in the park alone
until a parakeet flies over squawking.
Then alone again except for my dead friends
who always walk with me for company.

At that point Raven came in and said
"Look at all these people in the park
see how moving they are with their small joys
and sorrows, squabbling with each other
and their dogs. Weep," said Raven,
"open your heart and weep, it's the only response."

As I was sitting down on a bench
to follow instructions, Otter came in and said
"Stop! Don't waste your time here!
There are good Sardines waiting at home for lunch!"

Cold storage London

Clapton, East London

In January cold storage London
the bare plane trees between
my window and Canary Wharf
should leaf out four months from now

But the winter cold raises fundamental
doubts that move inside my body:
will the leaves in fact return
can I hold out until they do

The man I met in Hackney Marshes
in the cold today
told me of the birds
he'd watched there twenty years ago
reed buntings and goosander
all gone the yellowhammer
the long-eared owls no more

All we love dies or disappears
so I forgive myself
repeated pulses of anxiety
about whether the plane trees
will leaf out again next Spring

Hackney falcon

London

Because it was Christmas Eve
bicycles, dogs and their people
were absent from the path
towards Friendship Bridge and
the fields beyond.

Seeing him there, it took a while to riffle
through the mental files.
"They're vulnerable on the ground,"
a movie star's daughter, a falconer herself
told me years ago in a Buddhist retreat
"so you seldom see kestrels there."

He held the fresh vole in his talons
and parsed shreds as we approached.
Watching us he hawked it down
gorging on dark gobbets of entrail
warm red meat and blood
then finished hair, bone, tail.

Rising from the ground
he showed cinnamon wings
flew straight at us
then veered sharp away along the Lea.

All my neighbours' houses

Homerton, East London

The green rectangle behind my newly
acquired Victorian has hosted
eyefuls of birds in our first six months here:
cormorants and gulls and slim gray herons,
blue tits, robin and generous bellied
wood pigeons, invasive green parakeets
with their intelligent charms, crows, and swifts
chittering high above.

In the heat of this London summer
I've been noticing the chimney pots
on all my neighbours' houses
and reflecting on their contribution
to the first chapter of global heating.
Ah, there's the blackbird's song
whose variety always reaches deep.

Harvest of mice

Homerton, East London

The smallest rodents in Europe
are harvest mice.
Light as a two penny piece
with prehensile tails
good for climbing stalks of grain.

White of Selborne says "they never
enter into houses" but we've found
four in ours in Hackney in the last three days.

Early this morning we walked
to the marsh to release one into tall grass.
We couldn't breakfast while our visitor worried.
When we caught the first, I didn't know
what kind of mouse it was and had to look it up.

Hoping I had a dormouse
I found myself thinking of nuts and honey
half-remembering Roman recipes.

Shoreditch

London

It's 6:12 a.m. and my taxi's
on Shoreditch High Street
pointed at Gatwick
news of a terrorist attack in London
the morning's radio.

I'm on my way to Stockholm
to work the bank holiday.
You got up early to make us
turmeric porridge with blueberries
and jasmine tea.

It's a tearing
a soft tearing
parting

In a neat hand

Homerton, East London

The damp paper on my front walk this morning
when I went out to meet the taxi
was a vocabulary exercise in a neat hand.
'Leveret' caught my eye, a term
in my own linguistic long grass.
Where I come from hares are jackrabbits
and their young are babies in the common speech.

Tonight in Stockholm's long twilight
returning to my hotel a shape—long ears, white tail.
They're now vanishing in Britain
where three quarters of a million are shot each year
including pregnant and nursing mothers.

So I was encouraged and given a space
remote, for a moment, from daily brutality
by my Swedish hare.

The Nightingale Doesn't Sing
Here Anymore

London

I hear the birds no longer here
I sense the life that has been lost
in these twenty short years
I've walked English countryside
lapwings and larks, yellowhammer and snipe
turtledoves and nightingales
starlings even house sparrows

I feel their absence
but those born into this depletion
will not feel it
will take this absence as ordained
and feeling rich in sunshine
may not act to change it
or know their poverty

Samphire summer

London 1995

It was the bar tailed godwits
lunging for lugworms
the reed bunting
clutching the stem
beak full of dragonfly
for the chicks.
It was feeding Victoria
sponge to the sparrows.

It was the fourth year
we've raided north
to the Yorkshire coast
for samphire, and we
nibbled it raw and gorged
on it cooked.

But most of all it was
the flooding and puddling
and pooling into
each other after.

My teapot

Homerton, East London

A spider's set up house in my teapot
casting her silk to the wall.
She retreats into the spout.

What worries me is how
to feed her. The fruit flies
breeding in the recycling bin
are all eaten by the pitcher plants.

Fathers and sons

London

on a hot June day in London I meet
a former American vice president
over drinks

then stop in a café for dinner
and admire the tattoo of my Russian waiter
who explains the compass on his forearm
points to his search for life's meaning

in my progress through town
I notice three father and son pairs
boys aged about eight to ten
one pair white, one Chinese, one black

each of the pairs
as they walk along
holds hands companionably

Meeting seals

Lowestoft, Suffolk

Last night I met a seal. She was in a poem by Robert
Bly. He met her in Point Reyes in Northern California.
I was there for a book reading. A man from the audi-
ence gave me Bly's *Point Reyes Poems.* Back in England
I opened them. Earlier we'd walked the beach south
of Lowestoft where the dunes run wild.

Above the tideline we saw a seal sleeping.
She opened a wary eye. We moved on. Opening
her eye was the only effort our encounter
required. Bly's seal lay suffering from a black oil
scum. He visited his seal two days running and
on the second she was dead. Ours was plump
and healthy.

Her refuge though is troubled. Day by
day the sea gets less friendly than any time
since her ancestors went back to the water
after mastering the land.

Lowestoft

Suffolk
6 Dec 2018

Gulls bawl and brawl and caterwaul.
They scream and skank and crowd you.
They mewl and skirl and laughabout.
They roustabout too and eat your chips and burgerends.

When you leave some fish from your fish and chips
they look up to acknowledge their god
after they've fought for the food.

Admire their reign while we have them
and know their perfect aim
on the day when my great aunt
her arms full of shopping looked up at the Sun
and a gull from a great height crapped square in her eye.

Praise them.

Dying at sea

After seeing a beach memorial of a drowning victim,
Lowestoft, Suffolk

the water was cold

no longer tho

the boat far away

so I'm returning home

blood as seawater salty

ocean

earliest ancestors

going home

now

home

Big moon tides

Lowestoft, Suffolk

In the time of big moons sandbars appear. The tide
falls extra low, big moon low, and the sandbars rise
from the sea beyond our window. North Sea sand
swept clean by waves. It's a new country. Gulls come
first. They don't hunt or fish just stand and walk their
ephemeral domain. Gulls see things a long way off.
You don't query their arrival.

It's the seals make you wonder. Gray and harbour
seals who ruck up then turn round to face the wind
and waves. Up to twenty of them. They relax like a
balloon lost half its air. How do they track the coming
of the strand. Do they lay plans, enjoy anticipation in
the planning.

It's only for a few hours it emerges but worth know-
ing. Freedom from dogs and people. Freedom from
the need to balance flesh against northern waters.

They stay near the edge. The best part is the game of
turning tides. There's not a Canute in the herd. They
look amused, maybe relieved when the sea comes in
to float them. Then they're gone.

Little terns

Lowestoft, Suffolk

Insistent wingbeats up from Africa to sand eels and breeding. Some nest straight on shingle south of Lowestoft. They've tuned themselves to rhythms of sand eels and pebble beach for millions of years.

Natural selection's honed them close to the edge—long migration, hard foraging, rough nesting—where there's nothing left to spare. Survival tabulated in small strokes—this female survived to breed with this male—then inscribed in genes. Nature does not look ahead so could not lay down in genes strategies to blunt our impact when we walked recent into their life.

Now little terns as fast declining.

Volunteers watch the colony all day long and ask dog owners to control their pets for the three minutes it takes to walk past the vulnerable birds and many do. Between 50-60 times a year though, a volunteer told me today, the

        dog owners ignore the explanations
        and let their pets run right through.

    if only they could see with open eyes
    open their eyes and they'd see
    there is wonder in this nesting site
    during nesting time there is wonder
    on this ordinary stretch of windy shingle
    a wonder such small birds such very small birds
    fly so far to land here so far to land right here
    to enact life's greatest traditions right here
    where I live how lucky I am to live here now
    for them to nest here now on this hard shingle
    how much harder a life they have than mine
    how seeing them calls up reverence
    from my gut from my head from my memories
    from ancient parts of me they connect
    how this reverence spills over into my life
    till I appreciate my life and the life of all life

A pair of terns that's disturbed stops breeding for the
year, so their numbers keep plunging. Some years
the colony has no young at all. The nesting terns'
acute evolved reflex sees galumphing dogs as hungry
wolves. Kids running through don't disturb them half
as much.

Beach goers want dog free beaches too, so increasingly dogs are not allowed near swimmers and their kids, and dog owners seek wilderness beaches.

The dogs can't be expected to understand. What about people spoken to kindly and patiently by volunteers. Three minutes as they walk past.

how can we reach them
help them understand
three minutes of awareness for the terns
would reach down
to heal their own rages and aches and sorrows

how reach them when they shout obscenities
at kindly volunteers
since reaching them
would help heal the world

it's more than these terns too it's all the
species of birds all around the world all of
those who nest on shingle or sandy beach

plummeting in numbers all these birds
millions of years older than us

if we don't act
all of them
will be
gone soon
all of them
all of them
all of them
if we don't act
and then
from
whom
will
our
descendants
learn

The sitting still year

Lowestoft, Suffolk

The sitting still year of corona virus
we've been on North Sea's coast

walking the shore
learning sea rhythms
and the lifecycle of kittiwakes

Hongzhi Zhengjue's dictum
'merge your mind with cosmic space'
has been both comfort and challenge

But when North Sea gales howl cold
at 45 miles an hour gusting to 60

I recall our warm times
these last three decades
in the foothills of the French Pyrenees
near the Mediterranean
tucked in our goathouse
walking the hills, drinking local wine

on mange bien ici
one of our neighbours likes to say
while warm winds atomize
oils from garrigue herbs
then introduce them to the room

Blues and strands and islands

To Beijing from London late afternoon
the North Sea slices the clouds back
to blues and strands and islands
and it comes easy the thought
at the end of the week we converted
our civil partnership to marriage
stretching, backdated, eight years now
that it runs deeper than ever
and the edge of this ever will keep
disclosing as it moves forward like
the Sun racing across the face of Earth
the blues and strands and islands
of who we together are

Beijing music

In Beijing's Beihai Park
I'm one of thousands.
The air is cleaner than normal.

I'm sitting in the shade
as azure winged magpies
live their life around me and
a mix of music is in the air.

A woman screeching
hits from Chinese opera
over a recorded soundtrack
to an appreciative crowd
a jazz horn playing on her aural
edge and a fiddler with
two strings near my shady hut.

For a moment the wind
comes up and the trees' leaves
make the dominant sound.

Festival of Cuckoos

Beijing

With the parasite's sense of secrecy
cuckoos are seldom seen
but today by a lake in Beijing
in the Olympic park
at least six males were flying and calling
and fighting to defend
territory and secure mates.

So many shows how well stocked
with birds suitable for surrogate
cuckoo parenthood this park is now.

Rhino poaching viewed from Beijing

Beijing

I'm back in Beijing with supreme court judges
from around the world

at the request of the Supreme People's Court
to train judges and prosecutors

Slides from a justice of the South African Supreme Court
show an endangered rhino

dead, its horn hacked off, to sell in Asia
a fake aphrodisiac

In the next day's news, a poaching story:
AK-47's and an axe, tools for rhino killers

were found near jumbled bones
of two men, or maybe three

it was hard to tell, since the pride of lions
they ran into while poaching rhino

had eaten every scrap of them, leaving
just a few bones near unused guns and axe

In the Beijing Airport

The beggar in the Beijing airport
came up to me.

Uncomfortable
I looked away and he walked off
limping.

Then realizing how
much harder his life is than mine
I put a fifty renminbi note in my pocket
in case I met him again.

Just after checking
in I saw him and watched
his joy as I gave him the bill.

Later
I was stopped when boarding
and upgraded to business class.

Slouching towards Ulan Bator

There's a sea change in Beijing
about protecting the Earth.
I gave a seminar this week to members
of the Supreme People's Court
on climate change cases:
they want to decide big ones.

Last visit was a seminar
on how to write a law to let
local NGOs sue companies.

Over lunch the senior judge:
"Please bring your work here.
It would be good to work with you."

Years ago, before I moved to LA
my old Zen teacher Maezumi Roshi:
"Can't you find some work to do down here?
There are a lot of problems."

That invitation led me to found
the LA office of NRDC.

This new request
from a senior Supreme Court judge
in the world's oldest empire—
where will this one take me?

Over the Gobi

It looks like lakes
refreshing and blue
enough to green the desert

but is instead
the contour of cloud shadows
on sand
in the unremitting sun

Grateful

I'm grateful to be in this plane over Ulan Bator
to have met with the Supreme People's Court
to have met with a senior environment minister for a
      private dinner on National Day
to have contacts in China more effective than in the
      EU or US
to be able to offer help to the planet
to research my deep hopes
to be able to try to realize them
to have a growing team of partners to do this with

On the Peak

Hong Kong

Being on the Peak thirty
years later in Hong Kong
I remember my parents.

I met them in this town
when they were coming out of China
and I Tibet. The black kites
soared aerobatically then too.

Temple of Literature, 11th Century

Hanoi

In a city of seven million
with five million motorbikes
it's hard to cross the street
or fill your breath

But in the Temple of Literature
it's quiet. Stelae ride stone
turtles in the garden

And carry vanishing glyphs
of doctoral candidates from when
this was the imperial university

In the sanctum is an altar
for Confucius, flanked by his main
disciples, incense billowing

Bowing to the Master
feeling connected with his lineage
I vow to study the Analects

Then walking around Lake Hoàn Kiếm
we pass a two-storey picture of Uncle Ho
looking young and handsome

A group of students stops us
eager to practice English
their teachers all of twenty

When they ask us to sing
Martin belts out 'Seven Lonely Days'
I coax a girl and she reveals
a traditional song with passion

The young male teacher thanks us,
says, do you have a relationship,
and winks

Daintree River

Queensland, Australia

dawn on the Daintree
before Sun finds its heat

tree-high hibiscus open
dark-holed yellow blooms
they'll drop on the water at dusk

a little kingfisher
second smallest in kingfisherdom
flashes blue and white when diving

eyes-over-waterline crocodile
large male nursing wounds red
from a fight over the girl

above on dark wings
first one seen here in years
wedge tailed eagle

Cassowary dad

Cairns, Australia

the largest land animal in Oz
their bloodline therapods like T rex
I had to meet them

days of tracking
much of their rainforest now suburb
carved down for dog and lawn

it took a week, scat in the forest
then blue fruit, cassowary plums
their favourite

cassowaries sow the rainforest
the seeds in their scat
the ones that grow

then one morning he came on six feet tall
body all black then head and neck mixed red and blue
bonelike crest above

every inch a dinosaur
with a velociraptor's slashing spur
in case you cross him

he brought along three babies striped like fawns
he'd nursed on the nest
since the female walks away once she's laid the eggs

babies he takes on daily feeding rounds
like he's done with each year's brood for forty years
and his male forebears tens of millions

from his long life of caring
one chick may make adult
the forest continuously downed around them

he eats nothing
until the babies have had their fill
then moves them wary
the ancient master
into narrowing rainforest shadows

Sarus and Brolga

Queensland, Australia

Queensland's Atherton Tablelands, higher
and richer than most of this nutrient poor continent
has an ancient crater miles wide
known as Bromfield Swamp.

At dusk near the end of winter, cold
we wait to see two kinds of crane
Sarus and Brolga, come in for the evening.

Brolga, grey with a red head,
are doing well in Australia and New Guinea
where conditions in their range have been kind.

They use their long beaks to hunt
for tubers and small animals, and live
in family groups, combining these to flock.

Sarus are taller, tallest of flying birds,
are elegant in gray, with a smaller dollop
of red on the head than Brolga.

Sarus lived in India and all southeast Asia
but have lost much of their range to our use of land
and are less than a tenth the strength

they stood in the nineteenth century. The British
in India liked to shoot them. Corrupting their Hindi
name 'sarasa', they called them 'serious' and 'cyrus'.

Maybe it's easier to murder something
When you don't call it by its true name.
When one of a Sarus pair was shot the partner

trumpeted its grief for days on end
and the Indians, who hold them sacred, say the grieving
bird would starve itself to death.

They are such a model of fidelity
newlyweds in Gujarat are still taken out to meet them.

Tonight a few of these Sarus come in with the Brolga.
they fly in swift and drop long legs like landing gear

A group is spooked by a wedge-tailed eagle coming
        in low.
They circle round the crater then land and both kinds
        of crane
mixing amiably, think night thoughts.

Save the Song

New South Wales, Australia

Rainforest, New South Wales. Looking for Superb
Lyrebird, musical genius. It's courting season now
and males show off. I've been studying: How boy
birds train. Learn from older guys. Practise for hours
honing personal style. How they mimic any sound
they hear. How they have the most complex song of
any bird. How they clear a stomping ground to show
off their dancing. How they work on their chops.
These song and dance men.

Alone in the forest we move quiet. Stop at an over-
look. A lone male belts out to fill the valley. Far away
but louder than a mezzo in a concert hall. Like he has
an amp.

We brim with his voice. It becomes clear: Save the song.

To hear it is to want to save it.

To save it is to save the forest and watershed.

Is to save the natural world in New South Wales. Is to save Australia. Is to stop global heating. Is to awaken people. Is to change our culture. Is to save civilisation.

Save the song.

Let it be loud. Let it be clear: Save the song.